THE AUTHOR'S GUIDE
TO CHOOSING A PUBLISHING SERVICE

Read this guide to discover the three questions you MUST ask your self-publishing company before you hire them

1760 E. River Rd., Ste. 145, Tucson, AZ 85718
888-934-0888 • www.wheatmark.com

The Author's Guide to Choosing a Publishing Service

Copyright © 2014 Grael Norton. All rights reserved. No part of this book may be reproduced or retransmitted in any form or by any means without the written permission of the publisher.

Published by Wheatmark®
1760 East River Road, Suite 145, Tucson, Arizona 85718 U.S.A.
www.wheatmark.com

ISBN: 978-1-62787-043-6 (paperback)
ISBN: 978-1-60494-790-8 (ebook)

FROM THE DESK OF GRAEL NORTON

Dear Author,

Choosing a publisher for your book isn't easy. Why? Because you're bombarded with misleading advertising, confusing claims, and simply bad information from "lowest-priced" service providers and high-pressure salespeople.

It's pretty crowded out there too. By our estimate, there are more than a hundred companies of various sizes competing to offer publishing services to authors in North America alone.

The once-proud publishing industry—formerly dedicated to bringing great books by great writers to eager readers—is flooded with fly-by-night self-publishing companies that sell shoddy editing, poor book design, and nearly worthless book marketing services.

The proof is in the pudding, as they say. The marketplace is flooded with books of laughable quality. Readers have a harder and harder time discovering great new books, and new authors have a harder and harder time breaking through the clutter and getting noticed.

How do you find a qualified, competent, and professional book publishing service? You start by reading this consumer guide. In this fact-filled report you'll discover the three different kinds of publishing (and how to decide which method is right for you), five costly misconceptions about publishing a book, and nine critical mistakes to avoid when choosing a publishing service.

Wheatmark was one of the pioneers in the modern publishing-services industry. We opened our doors in 1999, and since then we've published more than 1,500 titles by more than 1,000 authors. Over the course of those nearly fifteen years in business we've also counseled, coached, and trained countless authors about successful book publishing and effective book marketing. This guide is the culmination of those years of hard-earned experience.

FROM THE DESK OF GRAEL NORTON

We wrote this guide to help you better understand the fast-changing world of publishing. Now, with this information, you can make an informed, intelligent decision. If you have any questions about publishing, you're invited to call us at 888-934-0888, extension 2.

We've dedicated our business to educating authors. We'll be happy to help in every way.

To your publishing success,

Grael

Grael Norton, Director of Marketing
Wheatmark, Inc.

TABLE OF CONTENTS

1. The Three Methods of Publishing — 1

1. Get a traditional publishing deal by licensing the exclusive publishing rights to your manuscript — 3
2. Self-publish your book (form your own publishing company) — 5
3. Enlist a publishing services company to publish your book for you — 7

2. How to Decide Which Method of Publishing Is Right for You — 11

Bonus Section: Four Misused Terms to Ignore when Researching How to Publish — 15

1. "Traditional publisher" — 15
2. "Subsidy press," "co-publishing," or "indie publishing" — 15
3. "POD publisher" — 16
4. "Vanity press" — 16

3. Five Costly Misconceptions about Publishing a Book — 17

1. Book publishing is the same as book printing — 19
2. A good goal is to break even — 21
3. Book wholesaling is the same as book distribution — 23
4. Publishing a book will make you famous — 25
5. Publishing a book will make you rich — 27

TABLE OF CONTENTS

Nine Critical Mistakes to Avoid when Choosing a Publishing Service — 29 ④

1. Taking advice from unqualified amateurs — 31
2. Hiring unqualified amateurs to publish your book — 34
3. Not checking publishers out—at least what their customers say about them online — 34
4. Choosing a publishing service based mainly on price—not on value — 35
5. Choosing a publishing service based on royalty percentages — 37
6. Choosing a publishing service based on the author's price for books — 39
7. Choosing a publishing service because they're the biggest — 39
8. Choosing a publishing service that doesn't provide wholesaling — 41
9. Publishing a book that doesn't meet bookselling industry standards of quality — 41

Three Questions to Ask Your Publishing Service Before You Give Them a Single Penny — 43 ⑤

1. Do I retain all rights to my work—including the work you do for me? — 45
2. Do you publish anything that comes your way? — 47
3. Do you offer a press release service? — 48

A 100 Percent Guaranteed, Risk-Free Offer to the Reader — 51

THE AUTHOR'S GUIDE
TO CHOOSING A PUBLISHING SERVICE

THE THREE METHODS OF PUBLISHING

1

THE THREE METHODS OF PUBLISHING

Before we can begin discussing the extraordinary opportunities and potential pitfalls of publishing in the twenty-first century, we have to make sure we're on the same page about the different kinds of publishing and the terminology we use to talk about them.

In today's publishing landscape, there are essentially three ways to publish your book:

1. Get a traditional publishing deal by licensing the exclusive publishing rights to your manuscript

2. Self-publish your book (form your own publishing company)

3. Hire a publishing services company to publish your book for you

None of these three routes is the ideal path for every author. Each route to publication has its advantages as well as its disadvantages.

Let's take a quick look at how to accomplish route number 1:

1 Get a traditional publishing deal by licensing the exclusive publishing rights to your manuscript

This route to publication is both the most straightforward and the most difficult. All you need to do is land an agent who specializes in your book's genre. Some agents specialize in fiction, others in nonfiction. Often, agents will be even more specific, focusing on western fiction or self-help books, for example.

How do you find an agent? It's simple: pick up the latest *Guide to Literary Agents* by Writer's Digest Books. Look for the agents in your niche or genre, and query them. (The *Guide to Literary Agents* also contains detailed info on writing an effective query letter.)

The reason this route is so difficult is because publishing houses only license the exclusive publishing rights to a tiny percentage of the manuscripts that are submitted to them each year by agents or authors—most sources put the exact figure at less than 1%.

And the reason these publishing houses license the exclusive publishing rights to so few manuscripts is because they lose money on nine out of ten titles they publish!

A great many authors begin their publishing quest by exploring the traditional route to publication before seeking an alternative. However, most authors are better off skipping this step entirely, because in the vast majority of cases, it's simply a waste of time.

Most authors who land an agent do so through a personal connection, which can take a lot of time to develop: six months, a year, two years, or even longer. Some good places to explore making these connections include writer's conferences, retreats, and workshops.

HERE ARE SOME ADVANTAGES OF LICENSING YOUR EXCLUSIVE PUBLISHING RIGHTS:

- You don't have to pay the publisher
- You'll be paid an advance against sales
- Good physical bookstore distribution
- Bragging rights

HERE ARE SOME DISADVANTAGES OF LICENSING YOUR EXCLUSIVE PUBLISHING RIGHTS:

- Getting a trade publishing deal is extremely difficult
- You can't build relationships with your book's readers if you never publish
- You lose control of your content
- Your publisher controls your relationships

These days, the year or five you might spend looking for an agent and then having that agent shop your manuscript to publishing houses in hopes of landing a deal is much better spent simply publishing your book yourself or with the help of a publishing services company.

That way, you can get on with building an audience for your work, which should be your primary objective anyway.

Another potential drawback of licensing the exclusive publication rights to your work is losing control over your content and, potentially, over your audience. In a rights-licensing deal, your publisher will control your book, your content, and your audience: not you.

However, your ultimate goal as an author should be to build an audience of readers with whom you have a *direct, ongoing* relationship. If you license the exclusive publishing rights to your work, who owns the relationships that sales of your book will foster?

- The publisher has a relationship with the bookstore (its customer)
- The bookstore has a relationship with its customers—your readers

Where does that leave you—the author? In many cases: nowhere, with no customers of your own. What you want to do is avoid the doomsday scenarios where your publisher decides to delay your book's publication (sometimes for years, even) or unceremoniously dumps it on the market with little or no promotion (it happens all the time), and so kills your career.

There are very, very few circumstances where you want to give someone else this much power over your career as an author. Fortunately, these days, you don't have to. Let's turn our attention to publication route #2: self-publishing.

2. Self-publish your book (form your own publishing company)

This is the DIY approach in its truest form and strictest sense, wherein you yourself are the publisher. Make no mistake: it's a lot of work, and there's a steep learning curve. First, you'll need to set up your own publishing company, which includes:

- Organizing your company
- Hiring editors, designers, and other production people
- Publishing your book
- Selling your book

You'll be responsible for all the creative activities (fun!), but also all the business activities (a lot less fun), such as buying a block of ISBNs (international standard book numbers), setting up distribution, and, of course, shipping books to retailers.

You may choose to hire a company or companies to do some of these tasks for you, or you may handle every last detail yourself.

There are some decided advantages to self-publishing. This may or may not include hiring a publishing services company to do some or all of the necessary activities for you.

HERE ARE SOME ADVANTAGES OF FORMING YOUR OWN PUBLISHING COMPANY:

- Complete control over your book's content
- Complete control over your book's layout and design
- Equal access to online sales channels
- Higher royalties/percentage of sale on each book sold

HERE ARE SOME DISADVANTAGES OF FORMING YOUR OWN PUBLISHING COMPANY:

- You assume the financial risk
- You need to make informed decisions to be successful
- You're responsible for generating sales
- You have limited access to the physical bookstore market

Another factor to consider is your time. If you start your own company, be prepared to put as many hours into your publishing project as you would into a (nearly) full-time job.

Moreover, you won't be spending all your time doing the two most important activities you should be doing as an author: writing and marketing. That's why we don't recommend this route to most authors—and in particular, to first-time authors.

Here's the ultimate warning about self-publishing (doing everything on your own): while the creative part of the project can be fun and liberating, that's only a small part of the publishing process. The business side of things is where all the money is made—or lost.

Unfortunately, writing a book does not qualify you to handle the business side of things. The skills required to put a pen to paper are very different from those required to run a business (much less a *profitable* business): marketing, sales, distribution, customer service, accounting, etc. Many authors jump into self-publishing with little thought given to this critical point.

Recall that traditional publishers are finding it very hard to make money these days, and most independent bookstores are struggling. Even large bookstore chains are declaring bankruptcy and going out of business!

How do you plan to do better than these traditional, professional players? If you don't have a ready answer, consider the third route to publishing:

3 Enlist a publishing services company to publish your book for you

Essentially, publishing services companies aggregate all the services noted in #2 above for their author clients. A single investment ranging from a few hundred dollars to tens of thousands of dollars gets you a published book.

This third publication route is frequently referred to as "hiring a self-publishing company," but this is a bit inaccurate as in just about every case, the publishing services company owns the ISBN—which makes that company the publisher of record—so technically, you are not "self-publishing." (This is neither an inherently bad nor an inherently good thing, but again, it's worth clarifying so that we're all on the same page.)

There are as many variations of publishing services companies as there are flavors of ice cream at your local supermarket. Each has its own plans, pricing, and business models. One way to make some headway on this decision is to start by working on a budget (both in time and money) for publishing your book. Be both honest with yourself about what you can afford, and realistic about what you can accomplish with different budgets.

Today, you can publish a book for $0. Or you can publish a book for $1,000 . . . $10,000 . . . even $100,000. Generally speaking, you get what you pay for. A realistic budget for properly publishing most books (including solid editing and proofreading, an eye-catching cover, and strong interior layout) is between $4,000 and $6,000. (The variation lies in part in the amount of editorial and design work needed to make the book the absolute best it can be.)

Books that fall on the low end of the design-time scale, like novels, will be closer to $4,000 or $5,000. Books that are design-heavy, like business books with lots of charts and graphs, or textbook-type projects with lots of images, will fall into the higher range of $6,000 to $10,000.

HERE ARE SOME PUBLISHING SERVICE ADVANTAGES:
- Access to a one-stop shop of services including (in many cases) editing, layout and design, publishing, printing, wholesaling, order fulfillment, royalties management, etc.
- Single point of contact should any problems arise during the publishing process
- Someone else manages the business relationship with wholesalers (like Ingram) and retailers (like Amazon) for you

 HERE ARE SOME PUBLISHING SERVICE DISADVANTAGES:
- You give up some money on each book you sell
- Your cost for copies of your own book is generally higher
- Some publishing services companies have terrible contracts

Ultimately, how do you decide if self-publishing or working with a publishing services firm is right for you? All it takes is asking yourself three simple questions:

A. Do I know who my book's market is?

B. Do I know how to reach those readers? (Better yet: have I already begun doing so?)

C. Can I afford (both in time *and* money) to reach my readers when I'm published?

If you can answer yes to all three of these questions, then you should feel comfortable working with a publishing services firm to publish your book. If you can't, then you're not quite ready to publish your book, and may benefit from one of the services we have available toward the end of this guide—a Book Marketing Blueprint.

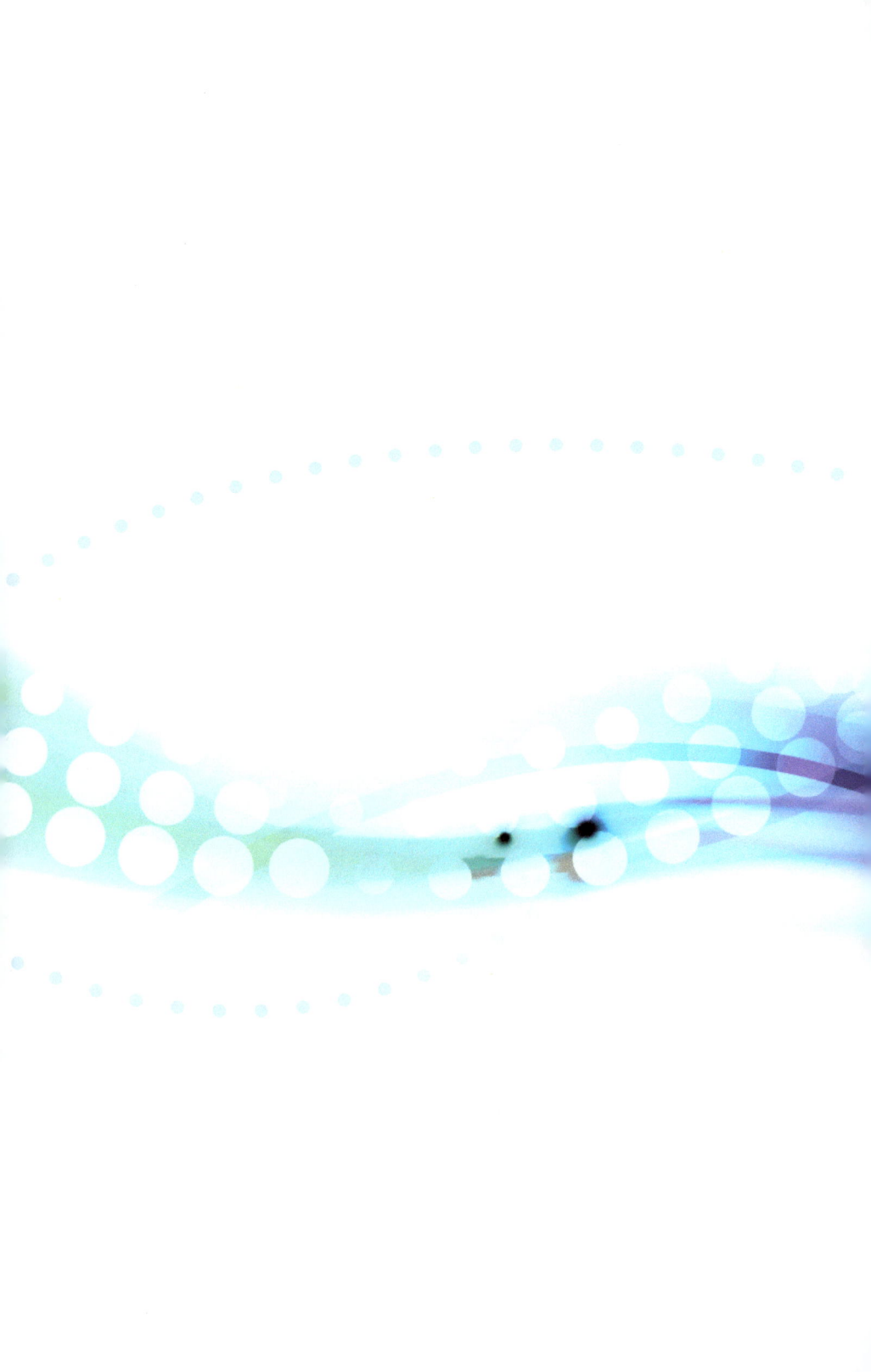

HOW TO DECIDE WHICH METHOD OF PUBLISHING IS RIGHT FOR YOU

2

HOW TO DECIDE WHICH METHOD OF PUBLISHING IS RIGHT FOR YOU

If prestige is the most important thing to you—and control of your book's content, design, and distribution is not—then the first publishing option, licensing the publishing rights to a trade publisher, is right for you.

 A WORD OF CAUTION:

Do not chase a trade publishing deal because you want your publisher to market your book for you. The vast majority of rights-licensing publishers are only interested in authors who have a sizeable existing platform and big plans to market their books. They don't like gambling on the unknown and usually won't. Moreover, they will *never* gamble on the lazy!

If total control over every aspect of the publishing process, including managing the back end of the business, is the most important thing to you, then self-publishing by forming your own publishing company is the right route to take.

 A SECOND WORD OF CAUTION:

You need to start learning as much about the business of publishing as soon as possible. A good resource for getting started is www.selfpublishing.com.

If what you want to focus on is writing and marketing—and that is exactly what the vast majority of authors looking to develop careers should focus on—then working with a publishing services company is the best way for you to publish, particularly if you're a first-time author.

> **A THIRD WORD OF CAUTION:**
> Most publishing services companies are perfectly adequate for someone publishing a noncommercial project such as a family memoir. However, many of these same companies are a liability when it comes to a project with commercial aspirations, and in some cases, working with these subpar companies can seriously damage your career.

The remainder of this guide will focus primarily on helping you to select a publishing services company that will be an asset to you and your books—not a liability—and will assist you with publishing properly so that you can build a lasting career as an author.

BONUS SECTION:
FOUR MISUSED TERMS TO IGNORE WHEN RESEARCHING HOW TO PUBLISH

In the course of doing research about how to publish your book, you're likely to come across some terms that will confuse you, that will be unclear, or that you will see used in different ways by different sources. Here are some publishing terms to take with a giant grain of salt:

1. "Traditional publisher"

If a publishing company identifies itself as a "traditional publisher," it probably isn't. (Random House and the other Big Six publishers never refer to themselves as "traditional publishers.") There's usually some sort of catch, or the company wouldn't market itself this way.

PublishAmerica fits this category. Its business model is to offer free publishing services to authors in exchange for the exclusive publishing rights to their work for a certain number of years (seven, the last time we checked). PublishAmerica makes its money by selling its authors copies of their own books at a significant premium. While we don't have a problem with companies offering publishing services to authors in any way they see fit (it's a free country), mischaracterizing what business they are in is a different matter. Proceed at your own risk!

2. "Subsidy press," "co-publishing," or "indie publishing"

A "subsidy press" provides publishing services to authors. The same is true with a "co-publishing" or an "indie publishing" company, which is the nomenclature of choice for Author Solutions and its brands, including AuthorHouse, iUniverse, Trafford Publishing, Xlibris, and its white-label brands WestBow Press, Balboa Press, Abbott Press, and many, many others. Author

BONUS SECTION:
FOUR MISUSED TERMS TO IGNORE WHEN RESEARCHING HOW TO PUBLISH

Solutions runs these latter companies and splits the profits with their trade-publishing parents.

Ultimately, it's important to bottom-line these companies for what they are: companies that provide publishing services to authors. Don't be fooled by claims of association either—working with one of the above-mentioned white-label companies does not in any way improve your odds of getting a traditional publishing deal. They're doing it for the money, period.

"POD publisher" 3

There's no such thing as a "POD publisher." POD (print-on-demand) is a combination of printing and fulfillment technologies, and publishing services companies do not have a monopoly on their use. Major trade publishers, publishing services companies, and self-publishing authors all use this technology to their benefit when appropriate. In fact, if this label were accurate, Simon and Schuster would be the largest POD publisher in the world!

"Vanity press" 4

People who claim that no one can be successful working with a publishing services company, despite plenty of evidence to the contrary, use this term almost exclusively in a derogatory sense. You should ignore this label because the person using it almost always has an agenda that is unrelated (or even in opposition) to your agenda: getting copies of *your books* sold and building *your career* as an author. In every other case, their agenda is to sell you something.

FIVE COSTLY MISCONCEPTIONS ABOUT PUBLISHING A BOOK

3

FIVE COSTLY MISCONCEPTIONS ABOUT PUBLISHING A BOOK

The following five misconceptions can cause you massive (and potentially expensive) headaches over the course of your publishing project:

1) Costly misconception number one: Book publishing is the same as book printing

One of the most basic misconceptions about publishing a book is that the activity is synonymous with printing a book. Actually, printing is just one of the steps in book publishing.

Before printing, there is market analysis and positioning, editorial review, editing, interior design and layout, proofreading, cover design, ISBN assignation, LCCN assignment . . . and a whole host of other activities. This is true of any book you hope to sell in a competitive environment, such as your local bookstore or online bookstores such as Amazon.com.

Not only is printing a book one of the last steps in the publishing process, but it can also be one of the least complicated. While printing is certainly important, it is by no means what makes or breaks a publishing success.

And yet, many authors base their entire publishing decision on this step. They spend most of their time comparing print prices and methods (such as digital versus offset, 1,000 copies versus 5,000, and so on) when in fact, they've missed or skipped some very important steps in the process—steps that often separate the books that become publishing successes from the tens of thousands of failures published every year.

That said, knowing about the different kinds of printing can give you some insight into some of the potential pitfalls of publishing and help ensure that your project becomes one of the few standouts.

Here are some quick-and-dirty definitions about printing processes:

- **Offset printing.** Printing using older, film-to-plate technology. Usually you'll need to print at least 2,000 copies of your book to make this method of printing cost-effective.

- **Digital printing.** In this scenario, copies of your book are printed using newer, digital-file-to-plate technology. Print runs can be smaller—even a single copy at a time.

- **Print-on-demand.** This technology combines digital printing with automatic order fulfillment so books can be printed, packed, and shipped as needed via an automated system. This technology has revolutionized the publishing services industry by making it easier and more cost-effective for authors to get their work in print.

Today, many authors work with publishing services companies to publish their books. It's so much easier now than in the old days when self-publishing authors would be forced to invest thousands of dollars in a print run while not having meaningful distribution in place. Today's independent author doesn't need to spend all that money on printing, so many don't.

But this is also where it all goes so terribly wrong for many of today's authors.

Perhaps because they don't have to invest thousands of dollars in printing, many authors underfund their project. They publish subpar books that are unedited or poorly edited with little thought given to the design or function of their books.

This casual attitude about quality is *fatal* to a project with commercial aspirations.

> **INSIDER'S TIP:** Even if you plan to use print-on-demand technology to print your book, pretend that you're about to invest an additional $10,000 in a large print run of 5,000 copies. That should put you in the right mind-set to ensure that you publish a high-quality book that's been professionally edited and designed.

The same is true with an e-book, in which case there may be no physical copies of the book printed at the title's launch. Many people take this as permission to upload an unedited Microsoft Word file to Amazon.com. But just because you can doesn't mean you should!

Do e-book readers care less about the quality of what they're reading than print readers do just because they're not reading a physical book? Certainly not! Both types of readers expect the content they buy from an author to be of top quality, or they won't buy a book from that author again.

To summarize:

- While *printing* a book is cheaper and easier than ever (via digital or POD technology, for example), properly *publishing* a good book still requires an investment of money and/or expertise.

- For a commercial project, you need professional editors and designers.

- Even a good e-book requires an investment to properly publish.

② Costly misconception number two: A good goal is to break even

Many authors spend a great deal of time calculating the "break-even" point for their project, figuring that it's an essential benchmark to establish before committing to move forward with it.

How many copies of my book do I have to sell to break even? an author asks himself.

His thoughts are often dominated by his author discount schedule. After all, the difference between the price he pays for copies of his book and what he sells them for represents his gross profit, and the greater that is, the fewer copies of his book he needs to sell to break even.

But here's an insight that, while it may surprise you, will serve you well in your publishing project: forget about breaking even—at least in the beginning.

If you're going to properly publish a well-designed, well-edited, high-quality book simply for your friends and family, you're not going to break even.

And if you're publishing a book with commercial aspirations (i.e., you hope to sell thousands of copies at a minimum), then you need to invest the amount of money necessary to create a book that has the potential to compete with books published by trade publishers—a book that not only has the potential to sell thousands of copies, but also creates additional revenue streams for you (such as speaking engagements) by enhancing your reputation with your audience.

Here's an analogy. When you see the previews for a new movie at your local Cineplex, do you imagine that the film's producers are sitting around in Hollywood thinking, "Gee, I really hope we break even on this one . . ."?

Of course not—they're hoping to make money hand over fist. They've invested in the creation and marketing of the film to make that happen, too.

The same is true for your book: you need to invest whatever's necessary to get the highest-possible-quality product (within reason, of course) before even a single copy is printed.

FIVE COSTLY MISCONCEPTIONS ABOUT PUBLISHING A BOOK

> **INSIDER'S TIP:** Forget about breaking even. No one hits a home run in any business by bunting; invest what is necessary to create a top-quality book. Having a high-quality book is some of the best insurance you can buy to make your publishing project a success.

Then, launch your new book with POD technology or an e-book, and see how it's received. You may discover all kinds of wrinkles you never considered during the publishing process—the worst being that you haven't properly identified the market for your book.

What you ultimately want to avoid is the independent publisher's worst nightmare: 1,000 or 2,000 or 5,000 or 10,000 copies of your book sitting around collecting dust in the garage where you used to park your car.

Don't let that be you.

The *only* exception to this rule is if you have a presale commitment from a buyer or buyers for an agreed-upon amount of money and *the check has cleared the bank.*

To summarize:

- Printing a bunch of books without first test-marketing your product is a fabulous way to lose a lot of money—and for no good reason.

③ Costly misconception number three: Book wholesaling is the same as book distribution

This critical distinction escapes many first-time authors—mostly because publishing services companies do a poor job of educating them about it.

A book wholesaler is a company that wholesales titles (usually by stocking them) so that retailers, such as Amazon.com, your local independent bookstore, your town's Barnes & Noble, or your local university's college bookstore can order any book they want from a single source. Book wholesaling is a matter of efficiency—a one-stop-shop for bookstores.

> **INSIDER'S TIP:** Generally speaking, you do not need to work with a book distributor to get your book listed on online bookselling sites such as Amazon.com or BarnesandNoble.com. Wholesaling is adequate for this purpose.

In North America, Ingram Book Company and Baker & Taylor are two of the largest and most prominent book wholesalers. In the UK, Bertram is a popular book wholesaler.

A book wholesaler doesn't do anything to encourage bookstores to order copies of your book—that's the job of a book *distributor*.

A book distributor usually employs salespeople who call on the book buyers from chain and independent bookstores and pitch their catalog of titles. In exchange, the book distributor takes a percentage of sales from any titles it sells. Distributors provide one-stop-selling for publishers, in effect. In exchange for this convenience, distributors usually require the exclusive right to sell a publisher's titles—the publisher can't sell its titles separately on its own.

So why doesn't every book get connected with a book distributor? After all, aren't these the people who sell books to bookstores? Well, yes—except that these aren't the people who market to *readers* to get them to go to the bookstores to buy your book. That job—which is increasingly the responsibility of the author—requires money or time, and frequently, both.

To summarize:

- Wholesaling makes your book *available* to be sold; distribution is a function of selling your title to bookstores, but not to readers.

Costly misconception number four: Publishing a book will make you famous

When you publish your first book, you will be proud. And you should be. Not everyone has accomplished what you have.

A quick look at Amazon.com's site should help shatter the myth that publishing a book will make you famous. As of this writing, there are more than eight million books for sale on Amazon.com, and you've never heard of the vast majority of their authors.

These days, just getting it published isn't what separates a successful title from an unsuccessful title. Good marketing is what separates successful and unsuccessful titles.

Marketing has always been a bit of a controversial topic amongst authors, but today's publishing marketplace makes the reality clear.

It is absolutely critical to understand—before you publish your book—that your publisher will not be the primary driver of the marketing and sales effort for your book.

It doesn't matter if you license the publishing rights of your work to a trade publisher, self-publish, or work with a publishing service; you will be the primary factor driving the sales of your book.

Many authors respond to this reality by purchasing marketing services offered by publishing services companies, but be wary of hiring other people to market your book for you until you understand the result you can expect from those particular marketing activities.

Many authors spend thousands of dollars on vendors for marketing services, only to be disappointed when they sell few books, if any.

In many cases, this isn't the marketing vendor's fault—they may have done exactly what they promised to do. The fault lies instead with the author who didn't understand what outcome they could reasonably expect from the marketing activity in the first place.

The best antidote to this disappointment is to start investing in your own marketing education. You can pick up books about book marketing at your local bookstore or library.

> **INSIDER'S TIP:** Good marketing isn't like gambling—you don't just place your bet and pray. Take the time to learn about marketing, and the payoff in increased book sales will be enormous.

If you take the time to educate yourself about effective book marketing, you'll learn what's possible to do yourself. Then, if you need a vendor's help, you'll understand what you're buying and what you can reasonably expect the outcome to be.

Another good resource to check out is "The One Way to Market Your Book," a special Authors Academy presentation that you can register to watch for free at www.AuthorsAcademy.com. (Authors Academy is a service of Wheatmark.)

To summarize:

- Just because you publish it doesn't mean anyone will buy it.
- Good marketing is what sells books (and can eventually make you famous).

5   Costly misconception number five: Publishing a book will make you rich

This goes hand in hand with costly misconception number four, that publishing a book will make you famous.

The truth is, it's very hard to get rich selling books. Most authors with trade publishing contracts are thrilled to get a $10,000 advance against royalties these days, if they get an advance at all. Once they earn out their advance (by selling enough books to cover the advance the publisher paid them), they might make $1 more in royalties for every additional book sold.

Meanwhile, authors who publish with publishing services companies may make two or three times as much per sale: $2, $3, or even $4 a book, and authors who self-publish (form their own publishing companies) may make even twice as much as that on each sale.

But even if you somehow manage to make $10 on every book you sell, you'll need to sell 5,000 copies of your book *per year* just to gross $50,000 and make a modest middle-class living.

Yet many of the most successful trade-published authors we know top out at 10,000 copies sold per title, period. They're certainly not making a living from their book sales!

Then there are the independent authors. Wheatmark's own sales-recognition program, Great Expectations, formally recognizes our clients' sales achievements at 2,000 copies and 5,000 copies sold.

Those aren't easy sales figures to hit. According to the Science Fiction & Fantasy Writers of America, the average title from a publishing service sells less than 200 copies.

It's safe to say that publishing a book is not a good plan for getting rich.

INSIDER'S TIP: There are a few outliers in self-publishing who've managed to make a small fortune through book sales alone—often by selling large numbers of e-books before selling their print publishing rights to a trade publisher. In every case, these authors made significant investments in professional editing, design, and marketing. Even electronically, publish properly!

But while publishing a book or books alone is not a great way to make money, you can make a lot of money as a result of being a published author.

The opportunities are nearly endless and include such activities as licensing your content for other media and other markets (foreign and translation rights), merchandising, speaking, and delivering info products and coaching programs.

To summarize:
- There are much, much easier ways to get rich than selling books.

NINE CRITICAL MISTAKES TO AVOID WHEN CHOOSING A PUBLISHING SERVICE

4

NINE CRITICAL MISTAKES TO AVOID WHEN CHOOSING A PUBLISHING SERVICE

For this section of the *Author's Guide*, we're going to assume that you want to publish a book that competes with other titles already for sale in the marketplace.

We're not going to assume you want to sell a million copies, but we are going to assume that you'd like to sell at least 2,000, 5,000, or 10,000 copies to start with.

By the standards of the publishing services industry, that would make your book a big success. By the standards of a trade publisher, 10,000 copies sold in a year would probably put you in the game for a publishing deal for your next book, if you wanted one.

So now that we've defined the rules of engagement, let's check out the nine critical mistakes to avoid when choosing a publishing service:

1 Critical mistake number one: Taking advice from unqualified amateurs

This almost shouldn't have to be written. We could just as easily say, "Don't believe everything you read on the Internet."

While it's a good idea to study a variety of resources before you publish your book, it's important to consider the sources of information you find, as well as the degree of experience of the people who offer it when you decide whom to work with.

People have a bad habit of believing the first opinions they come across, regardless of whether they are qualified opinions from those with deep experience in the subject.

But as you begin your publishing quest, some people will give you inaccurate or self-serving information. Others will mislead you, while others will use your relative ignorance to outright steal from you.

Here are the five types of people whose opinions you should totally ignore when it comes to making a decision about how to publish your book:

- **Commission Chris.** Popular at some of the big publishing services companies such as the Author Solutions brands, Commission Chris is the sort of person who's been on the job only a few months and knows next to nothing about commercial publishing. Commission Chris's goal is to get you to sign on the dotted line so he can make his commission, pay his bills, and move on to the next prospect. His only point of leverage is to discount the price of his company's package. (All that a discounted price indicates is that the service wasn't worth the full retail price in the first place.)

- **Unpublished Uli.** Uli wants more than anything to land an agent who can license the publishing rights to his work to a publisher. He spends his days attending writers' conferences and trolling on message boards expressing his outrage at the publishing services industry and repeating inanities like "money should flow to the author." In some cases, Uli even has a publishing deal, but his disappointment at the lack of support he gets from his publisher causes him to lash out at enemies real and imagined. He doesn't give credit where credit is due to an author who puts her money where her mouth is and goes out and makes her publishing project a success herself, either by self-publishing or by working with a high-quality publishing services firm.

- **One-book Wanda.** Wanda went into the publishing business after publishing her first book on CreateSpace or Lulu. The cost of working with these companies is low, but the know-how required to do a great job is quite high, so she spots a business opportunity and hangs out her shingle. However, simple technical know-how with template cover design generators does not a successful publishing project make. Unless Wanda's first book sold 10,000 copies, she likely has less knowledge about how to publish a successful book than you do if you've read this far in this guide!

- **Indie Ida**. Ida believes in the DIY ethic to a fault. She grows all her own food and can't imagine why an author wouldn't want to handle every last detail of their publishing project themselves. Well, Ida, some people like to grow their own food, some people like to shop at the grocery store and cook, and others like to eat at restaurants. The same is true with publishing services: not everyone wants to start their own publishing company, and by no means should everyone do it. In fact, the vast majority of authors are much better off not starting their own company—especially at the beginning of their publishing careers (see page 13). To complete the analogy: Imagine eating dinner at a nice restaurant. Now imagine *running* the restaurant. That's the difference we're discussing here.

- **Predatory Pete**. This is the worst character of them all. Predatory Pete feeds on the dreams of authors and exploits them at every opportunity. He engages in shady business practices such as connecting an author with an agent, only to have that agent request an up-front "reading fee"  (no legitimate agent requires a reading fee). Predatory Pete changes the name and location of his company frequently, as he's often only one step ahead of the law. Avoid him at all costs!

Critical mistake number two: Hiring unqualified amateurs to publish your book

This one's just plain *sad*. The number of books we've come across over the years that were poorly published by amateurs—usually by the authors themselves, but sometimes by people claiming to be professional publishing services companies—is shocking.

All you have to do is look at the covers and interiors of a few of the books a company has published. If they don't look pretty much like the books you see for sale in your local bookstore, find a different company to work with.

Don't wait to learn from booksellers or your readers that your book is subpar—that's too late.

Critical mistake number three: Not checking publishers out—at least what their customers say about them online

This is truly the Internet age, so there's no longer any excuse for doing business with unscrupulous characters.

At the very least, check out the companies you're interested in with the Better Business Bureau (www.bbb.org). It doesn't hurt to do a Google search of the company's name combined with the word "complaints" too, just to see what pops up.

If there are dozens (or even hundreds) of complaints, you may want to take that into consideration, especially if you read a bunch of complaints that seem reasonable.

Two notes of caution: First, some people just can't be satisfied. (If you own a business or work with customers in any capacity, you're already familiar with this.) Some customers complain about anything and everything, so their complaints should be taken with a grain of salt.

Second, some people have completely unrealistic expectations about publishing—in most cases because they didn't bother to educate themselves by reading a guide like this one, or *Self-Publishing for Dummies*, or other educational books and materials.

It's pretty easy to tell if a complaint comes from someone who didn't understand what they were doing in the first place when they engaged a company to publish their book for them.

At worst, the publishing services company did a poor job educating its prospective customers about what they could expect when working with them.

Fortunately, after reading this guide, this won't happen to you!

4 Critical mistake number four: Choosing a publishing service based mainly on price—not on value

This one is a biggie. As consumers, it's natural for us to consider price when making a buying decision.

After all, most of the products and services we buy seem like they're easy to compare: a plumber is a plumber is a plumber. You hire a plumber to fix the leaky faucet.

Though I'd argue that this isn't really the case—a good plumber is worth her weight in gold, while a bad plumber can cause you enormous headaches and expense—you can pretty much throw this idea out entirely when it comes to publishing services.

Why? Because when you choose a publishing services provider, you aren't just choosing a service provider—you're choosing a business partner to help make your project a success.

Publishing a book isn't the same kind of service as trimming your lawn, cleaning your house, or fixing your plumbing.

It's much more akin to buying into a franchise that (hopefully) helps you sell thousands of books and earn money from related products and services.

For example, every year people buy into a McDonald's or a Subway franchise to get into the restaurant business. They do so because these franchises are a proven system for making money.

What you get when you publish your book with a publishing service is help with creating your product (the sandwich or hamburger) along with back-end support similar to what the parent company offers to a franchisee (in our example, McDonald's or Subway).

Obviously, the goal in this system for the franchisee is to sell enough hamburgers or sandwiches not only to make a return on their investment, but to make a yearly profit as well.

Meanwhile, the more profit the franchisee makes, the more profit the franchisor (the parent company) makes, so the parent company has a strong incentive to see its franchisees succeed.

In publishing services, that means selling books—or at least furthering the author's career in some other (measurable) way that helps them make more money and be more successful. This requires specialized knowledge about publishing and marketing that takes years to acquire.

But shockingly few of the publishing services companies you'll find on the Internet know anything at all about selling books to *readers*. All you have to do is ask them how many copies the average title they publish sells, and you'll witness the depth of their expertise (or lack of it).

Their *actual* expertise is in selling expensive, useless marketing services to authors that don't result in readers actually buying their books! (For an example, check out the "Press Release Test" discussed later in this guide.)

While price should be a factor when choosing a publishing services company, don't make it your primary consideration—you're setting yourself up for failure.

Critical mistake number five: Choosing a publishing service based on royalty percentages

First off, keep your eyes peeled for false or misleading claims when it comes to royalties (more accurately identified as a percentage of sales). Some publishers claim to pay a "100 percent royalty," but this is meaningless until you check their actual numbers.

Publishers calculate their royalty rates based on different factors, so your best course of action is simply to ask for real, net numbers. How much in actual dollars will you make on each sale?

Here's what the math looks like on a typical 175-page paperback that Wheatmark publishes:

- Minimum retail price: $9.95 (set by us)

- Wholesale price: $7.96 (80 percent of list price)

- Author's royalty: $1.99 (25 percent of the wholesale price of the book)

That said, there's a real danger of giving this factor too much weight when choosing a publishing service. This goes back to the apples-to-apples comparison we mentioned above (or rather the plumber-to-plumber comparison).

Many authors request information from a number of publishing services companies, and then create charts so that they can compare things like royalty rates. Some publishing services companies even do this work for consumers by creating charts that compile these figures and posting them on their website or in a book.

Besides the fact that the information these sources provide is often inaccurate or out-of-date, there are two huge problems with this approach:

1. It assumes that the author and publisher are in competition with each other. In other words, the more money the publisher makes, the worse off the author is.
2. It assumes that the publisher hasn't earned the money they're making.

If either of these assumptions is true, then that publisher does not provide adequate value to its clients and is destined to go out of business eventually.

Rather than focus on how much money you make per sale, do everything you can to find a publisher who's invested in the outcome of publishing your book and their relationship with you as a client.

Ideally, that would involve a relationship that lasts many years and multiple titles because you're *both* making money from selling tons of books or growing your career in other profitable ways.

You don't want your publisher to go out of business. You want them to be there to support you in your career as an author for as long as you need and value that support.

Keep in mind that if a publisher publishes anything that comes their way, and works on dozens or even hundreds of projects simultaneously, they can't possibly give you or your book the attention you deserve when it comes to helping make your project a success.

We hear this complaint all the time from authors who've been persuaded by low-price offerings and high-pressure salespeople to publish with a company that ultimately abuses them and their work. These are some of the saddest stories around because they're lost opportunities.

INSIDER'S TIP: If you publish a bad book, you're not going to make any sales, so your royalty percentage becomes meaningless. 100 percent of nothing is nothing!

6 Critical mistake number six: Choosing a publishing service based on the author's price for books

This is a popular target of criticism from self-publishing industry "gurus." Mainly, they argue that companies shouldn't make a profit—or "too much" profit—from the books they sell to their clients.

But the only way a publisher should make little or no money from the sales of your books is when they don't provide a service for you. If that's the case, then they should simply design your book files and hand them over to you so that you can manage printing and fulfillment yourself.

That way, you keep all the profit because you do all the work—simple as that.

 INSIDER'S TIP: In nearly all cases where a publishing service claims they don't make any profit on the sale of your book, they own the printing company that prints your book, and that's how they make their profit. Don't be fooled by their supposed display of generosity.

7 Critical mistake number seven: Choosing a publishing service because they're the biggest

Many people prefer to do business with the biggest company they can find in a category because they figure the biggest must be the best. This is very poor reasoning when it comes to choosing a publishing service.

It's true that big companies (like the Author Solutions brands AuthorHouse, iUniverse, Trafford Publishing, and Xlibris) have economies of scale (and access to venture capital), so they're sometimes able to offer products and services to the public for less money than their smaller competitors.

But low prices are pretty much the only advantage the big companies have to offer their authors. Again, as we noted in critical mistake number five, a publisher that works on dozens or even hundreds of projects simultaneously can't possibly give you or your book the attention you need when it comes to helping make your project a sales success.

For example, the Author Solutions companies publish tens of thousands of titles a year—more than Random House, the United States's largest commercial trade publisher.

Again, as noted by the Science Fiction & Fantasy Writers of America, the vast majority of books published by these giant "author mills" sell 200 copies at most even though these companies have teams of people performing marketing services for their authors.

The above sales figures tell the real story: the big publishing services companies are in business to sell publishing and book marketing services to authors—not to sell books to readers.

We're sure the employees at these big companies are very nice, and we know they mean well, but they don't have a clue about what works and what doesn't when it comes to selling books.

In the best-case scenario, what you'll get when working with one of the big publishing services companies is a decent-quality book published at a fairly affordable price. This is great for a memoir or other personal project, but in most cases totally inadequate for a commercial project that will help lay the foundation for a lasting career as an author.

Critical mistake number eight: Choosing a publishing service that doesn't provide wholesaling

If you publish your book with a publishing services company that doesn't offer wholesaling (see page 23)—which means that they're essentially a glorified printer—you will be selling books out of the trunk of your car.

This isn't in itself a bad thing: many speakers and other professionals, for example, sell books in the back of the room when they speak or give presentations. They obviously need to have a supply of books on hand at all times.

However, there's really no reason why these sorts of professional authors shouldn't also have their books for sale on Amazon.com and other online booksellers. It's a great way to grow your audience, and it's basically free online advertising for your business on one of the web's most trusted sources of information.

In fact, people will usually buy your book from these online booksellers—so in effect, they'll be paying you to read your advertising!

For any other kind of author, the benefits of wholesaling should be clear—unless you really, really like driving!

 **Critical mistake number nine: Publishing a book that doesn't meet bookselling industry standards of quality**

If your stated goal is to publish a book that competes in the marketplace with any other book in its category, then you're in for a rough time if you make this mistake.

Industry standards of quality include professional cover and interior design, editing, and even physical book quality.

However, the vast majority of books produced by publishing services companies are of poor editorial and design quality.

On top of that, they're incorrectly priced for the markets they're supposed to sell into.

These books have *no chance* of ever being successful. They were destined for obscurity the day they were published.

In most cases, the author vastly overestimated what her publishing service could accomplish with a small or nonexistent budget for publishing. And in most cases, her publishing service did little to dispel her incorrect beliefs. They were simply happy to collect her money and call it a day.

The truth is, when you work with a publishing service to publish your book, you're essentially starting your own business. The product that you sell is copies of your book.

You've got to have a great product if you want to be successful.

Meanwhile, if you fail to meet at least the minimum standards, your project will fail, period.

Any company who willingly publishes a subpar book for you (after you've told them what your goals are) is ripping you off.

> **INSIDER'S TIP:** It's up to your publisher to watch out for you and to make sure you're publishing a book that meets the standards necessary to achieve your goal. Otherwise, they're just taking your money.

THREE QUESTIONS TO ASK YOUR PUBLISHING SERVICE BEFORE YOU GIVE THEM A SINGLE PENNY

5

THREE QUESTIONS TO ASK YOUR PUBLISHING SERVICE BEFORE YOU GIVE THEM A SINGLE PENNY

Most publishing services companies—or "self-publishing companies," as they're often called—can help you publish a well-edited, well-designed book.

The problem is, frequently they don't. Many companies will not be honest with you about what your project really needs to have a shot at being successful.

That's why it's so important to study resources like this guide so that you understand what's involved in publishing a book that competes with the best of them out there in the marketplace. So good for you for reading this far—you've already made a significant investment in your book's success!

Now that you know what's necessary to succeed when working with a publishing service, all that's left to do is to ask three simple questions to the publishing services companies you're considering working with.

These three simple questions are how you "bottom-line" these companies and figure out what their motivations really are. Are they an ethical publishing services provider, or not?

Whatever you do, don't sign a publishing agreement with anyone until you ask them!

1   Question number one: Do I retain all rights to my work—including the work you do for me?

This might seem obvious, and yet it's a chronic problem in the publishing services industry: an author hires a publishing services company to publish his book for him, but then signs away the exclusive publishing rights to his work in all formats and languages for a certain number of years.

This is crazy and could be easily avoided by simply reading the company's publishing agreement more carefully. If you don't understand the agreement, ask. If you don't understand the answer you receive, check with a lawyer or Mark Levine's excellent book on the subject, *The Fine Print of Self-Publishing*.

Here's the rule of thumb: When you hire someone to publish your book for you, you should retain all publishing rights, period. The publishing services company is performing services-for-hire for *you*, not licensing the exclusive publishing rights to your content.

If they are in fact licensing the exclusive publishing rights to your content, they should be paying you—not the other way around.

In addition, sometimes a publishing service will later tie up the deal you try to make with a rights-licensing publisher, either siphoning money off your deal or delaying your new publisher's ability to bring your work to market.

This is very sneaky and underhanded because the odds are that you were the primary force driving the marketing behind your book.

It was *your* effort that led this new publisher to be interested in licensing the exclusive publishing rights to your work, not the effort of your publishing service. Failing to acknowledge this fact is a shameless money grab.

Ultimately what you're looking for in a publishing services agreement is to grant your publishing services company the non-exclusive right to publish your work for as long as you want. You should be able to cancel your publishing agreement at any time for any reason, without any penalty whatsoever.

Ideally, you should also be able to take the production files of your book with you to your own publishing company or to another publisher—though unfortunately, in the case of some publishing services companies, the work may not be good enough to warrant taking with you.

Question number two: Do you publish anything that comes your way?

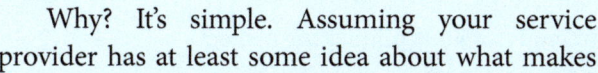

Here's a little nugget that will change the way you look at shopping for a publishing services company from here on out.

If your publishing services company does not have some sort of screening process in place to get new clients and new projects, they have no plans whatsoever to make money off the sales of your book.

Why? It's simple. Assuming your service provider has at least some idea about what makes a good book (factors that may include a well-defined target market, a strong title, great cover and interior design, being well written and edited, etc.), they'll do everything in their power to attract good books because that's how they will make money.

They'll also do everything they can to avoid working on bad books because that's a money-losing proposition for them.

If they have no plans to make money off the sales of your book, then they'll publish anything in any fashion because book sales aren't critical to their bottom line.

A quick glance at the online bookstore of just about every "self-publishing company" out there proves beyond the shadow of a doubt that they couldn't care less about your book selling ten copies, much less 10,000. The books are simply not of high enough quality, period.

We realize that this advice is the total opposite of all the other guides to self-publishing companies out there that urge transparency and what they identify as "author-friendly" practices such as publishing their prices on their websites.

In fact, this is the *exact opposite* of being author-friendly.

By publishing anything that comes their way, all these companies ensure is that they're going to publish a bunch of bad books by authors who take time and attention away from other, more worthy projects.

Furthermore, these companies create a negative publishing brand in the marketplace. Over time, allies such as your local chain or independent bookstore have learned to identify these publishing services companies as publishers of garbage and little more.

These bookselling allies are looking to make money-selling books. When they get inundated by requests from amateur authors with poor-quality books for shelf space, scheduled signings, etc., it's only natural for them to create a blanket policy refusing to work with all the authors from a particular publishing services company or any publishing services company.

If your publishing service doesn't interview you about your goals for your publishing project, and doesn't request to see your manuscript or at least a sample of your manuscript before they offer to publish your book, they don't expect you to ever sell a single copy.

Their business model is based on selling publishing and marketing services to authors—not on selling books. What do they care if you publish a bad book? It's on to the next ~~sucker~~ author.

Question number three: Do you offer a press release service?

This one's a trick question—a "gotcha!" Why do we recommend you ask it?

Success in any business endeavor boils down to first understanding and then applying effective marketing principles. The same is true with your book project: it's all about the marketing.

So why not hire your publishing services company to market your book for you by, for example, issuing a press release to the media about your book? After all, they know more about book marketing than you do, right?

Wrong.

It's easy to see from the services they offer that most publishing services companies either don't have a clue about how to actually sell books or are simply content to rip off their clients.

You'd think that after these companies helped their authors publish poor-quality, overpriced books—and made a profit doing so—they'd be satisfied, right?

Not even close!

As soon as they finish publishing a bad book, these same publishing services companies get their commission salespeople back on the phones to sell wet-behind-the-ears authors some truly atrocious marketing services.

We're talking about services that don't have a snowball's chance in Hades of helping authors achieve their goal of selling more books.

Wheatmark has a litmus test for judging if a publishing services company has its authors' best interests at heart when it sells them a marketing service.

We call it the Press Release Test.

Nearly all of the self-publishing companies out there sell a generic press release service to their authors. It usually involves having someone write a press release and blasting it out to 1,000 or 100,000 or 1,000,000 email addresses and fax numbers.

Sounds great, right? Think of all those people who are getting exposed to the news of your book's publication!

…Except for the blatantly obvious problem that seasoned marketers spot immediately: *publishing a book is not news.*

The day you publish your book, you'll feel like a million bucks. You'll feel like you've scaled Everest, and if you've published a great book, you have. You've accomplished something that most people only dream of accomplishing in their lifetime.

Unfortunately, proof of that same achievement is available eight million other times on Amazon.com alone—that's how many unique titles are listed there—and the list grows longer and longer every day.

Publishing a book is not news! Nobody cares that you published a book except your friends, your family, and your existing fans. Everybody else out there is listening to Zig Ziglar's radio station **WIIFM: What's in It for Me?**

> **INSIDER'S TIP:** Learn how today's smartest authors market their work by viewing "The One Way to Market Your Book," a special Authors Academy presentation you can register to watch for free at www.AuthorsAcademy.com.

If you want to connect with your book's readers, you're going to need to figure out how to get a marketing message in front of them that's all about *them*—not all about *you*, which is what a press release announcing the publication of your book is about.

A press release can be very effective as long as it's about something that actually qualifies as news.

You could send a release to your local paper's food section announcing the tapas-making workshop you'll be holding at a local Spanish restaurant where you'll also share never-before-revealed Catalonian cooking secrets from your newly published cookbook.

See how that works? *That's* the kind of news the media is looking for: information the paper's readers will actually be interested in learning about!

Don't be a victim of your own ego or your publishing services company's come-ons. Educate yourself about effective marketing first.

If you take the time to properly educate yourself about effective book marketing, you'll learn what's really possible to accomplish. Then hire someone to help, if you need it.

Marketing your book doesn't have to take a lot of money, but it will always take an investment of time and effort.

A 100 PERCENT GUARANTEED, RISK-FREE OFFER TO THE READER

Congratulations! If you've read this far, you've invested the necessary time to educate yourself about choosing a professional publishing service that will help you properly publish your book.

You're way ahead of 99 percent of authors out there looking to publish a book this year.

You know all about the general process of selecting a professional publishing services provider, as well as the specific questions to ask that will help ensure that you publish a book you can be proud of.

But what if you still have questions? What if you're still unsure how to publish? (Will you find an agent or self-publish? Will you publish in paperback, e-book, or both? Will you publish in audio?) Or perhaps you could use some more specific guidance about exactly who you should work with to publish your book.

In our experience, the best way to execute a complex publishing project is to plan it carefully from the very beginning, just like any other important project.

But most authors don't know how to go about making a plan to publish and market their books. There's so much information out there and so many options for editing, publishing, and marketing that it's easy to get lost. Where do you start?

We're here to help you plan a publishing project that succeeds. We've developed two solutions called a Book Publishing Blueprint and a Book Marketing Blueprint, and as a reader of this guide, you have the opportunity to sample one or both of these services risk-free.

Let's take a closer look at each one to see what it involves:

➔ Book Publishing Blueprint

Publishing a book can be an intimidating process. There are so many options, it's hard to know where to start! We've found that the best approach is to apply habit number 2 from Stephen Covey's *The 7 Habits of Highly Effective People*: begin with the end in mind.

When you work with us on a Book Publishing Blueprint, we'll set up a phone interview with you (or invite you to visit our offices in Tucson, Arizona, if you prefer) where we'll ask you a series of questions designed to help you clarify your goals for your project. Perhaps the most important is, *What is the ideal outcome for you with this book?* That's how we begin with the end in mind.

Your answers to these questions will help us guide you to select the appropriate formats, trim size, and publication methods for your title. We'll also be able to recommend what steps to take to get your manuscript into the best shape possible, as quickly as possible.

Once you're clear on your goals for your book and your reasons for publishing and have an understanding of how to prepare your manuscript for publication, you'll be crystal clear about how to proceed.

You'll dramatically increase the effectiveness of your publishing plan while significantly decreasing the amount of wasted time, effort, and money that you invest in your project moving forward.

➔ Book Marketing Blueprint

Each year, thousands of high-quality titles slip through the cracks of the public's consciousness. These titles could inform, enlighten, and entertain if only they could find their audience, but they never do.

Why? Most of the time it's because the author or publisher didn't do enough research into the book's market (or audience) before publishing it—and even more important, didn't do enough to start connecting with that market before the book was published.

The importance of understanding your book's market as well as beginning the outreach process in the months leading up to your book's publication cannot be underestimated!

Your Book Marketing Blueprint will help you zero in on the niche your book will sell into with laser-like precision. These days there are more opportunities than ever to start connecting with your target audience via the Internet.

You'll discover what to start working on now so that when you're ready to publish, there's a hungry audience ready and waiting to gobble up what you write!

➡ Book Publishing and Marketing Blueprint

If this is your first publishing project, this blueprint is for you. Having a detailed roadmap for how to publish and market your book will save you hours upon hours of time and potentially thousands upon thousands of dollars on your project!

A side note: If after working together on a Book Publishing or Book Marketing Blueprint we mutually agree to work further together on the project, your modest investment will be applied as a credit toward future Wheatmark services such as editing or publishing.

Regardless of whether or not we work together further on the project, we guarantee that you'll emerge from your blueprint session with a step-by-step roadmap to publishing and book marketing success.

We've already helped thousands of authors achieve book publishing and marketing success; now it's your turn!

Regardless of which service you choose, the risk is entirely ours

Regardless of which service you choose to work on with us first, you can feel confident knowing that all the risk at the beginning of our budding relationship is on our side.

Publishing a book is a very personal project. This is something you've been working on for months, if not years, and you want to see it brought into the world properly.

The right publishing counsel can help you do just that. The wrong publishing counsel can ruin your prospects for a successful career as an author!

That's why each of our blueprint services is backed by our **Unconditional, No-Wiggle-Room, Risk-Free Money-Back Guarantee**. If you're not absolutely thrilled with the quality of your Book Publishing or Marketing Blueprint, simply let us know and we'll refund 100 percent of your modest investment.

No conditions, no wiggling. No ifs, ands, or buts. 100 percent of your money back.

Ready to begin your own journey to publishing success?

The next step is for you to select either a Book Publishing Blueprint, a Book Marketing Blueprint, or a Book Publishing and Marketing Blueprint for your project.

Because of the amount of time they involve, we can only offer a limited number of Blueprint sessions to prospective authors each month, so don't wait to make this powerful investment in your publishing success!

Here are two easy options for getting started right away:

1. Place your order on our secure website here: http://www.wheatmark.com/blueprint

2. Call (888) 934-0888 (option 2) to place your order by phone.

We look forward to working with you on this critical first step of the publishing process!

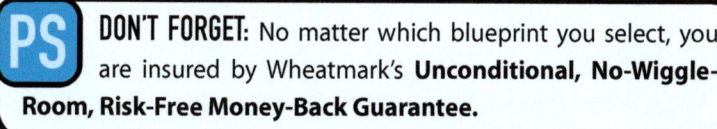

DON'T FORGET: No matter which blueprint you select, you are insured by Wheatmark's **Unconditional, No-Wiggle-Room, Risk-Free Money-Back Guarantee.**

FAQs (frequently asked questions)

Q: What do I do next?

A: To get started working with us on a Book Publishing Blueprint, a Book Marketing Blueprint, or a Book Publishing & Marketing Blueprint, please place your order securely on our website at http://www.wheatmark.com/blueprint or call us toll-free at (888) 934-0888 (option 2) to place your order by phone.

Q: What happens then?

A: As soon as we receive your order, we'll contact you to schedule your Blueprint session. If you're local to us in Tucson, Arizona (or if you like to travel), you'll be invited to join us at our offices for your session. If not, we can easily conduct your Blueprint session by phone instead.

Q: Do I need to have a completed manuscript to work with you on a Blueprint?

A: No. These services are ideal for clients who are still in the process of writing their books. Taking the time to properly plan your project in advance can pay off big time in terms of money and effort saved further down the line in the publishing process!

Q: What happens after we finish working on a Blueprint together?

A: If our Blueprint session reveals an opportunity for us to work together further on your project, we'll provide you with all the details of what we propose and how it will help you to achieve your goals.

Q: What's the typical investment for publishing a book with Wheatmark?

A: The typical investment for publishing a book with Wheatmark is $4,000–$6,000. This includes everything you need to make your book a success: editing, interior layout and cover design, and paperback (or hardcover) and e-book publishing in the six most popular formats.

Q: How long does it take to publish a book with Wheatmark?

A: Our publishing process generally takes about four months, depending on the services required to make your book the very best it can be.

Q: Why should I work with Wheatmark?

A: Wheatmark is the only selective publishing service with a proven marketing system, the Simple Marketing System, for helping our clients become bestsellers. Unlike other publishing services companies, we make the majority of our revenue from the sale of books—not services. This is simply because high-quality, smartly marketed books sell much better!

What folks have to say about working with Wheatmark

"I have been very, very pleased with the professionalism and support Wheatmark provides—including the Authors Academy. The first new novel I published with Wheatmark has sold five times as well as my previously published novels."

—Helena Schrader, Virginia
author of the Leonidas of Sparta trilogy

"I know how to write, but I'm a novice at this marketing stuff. Your honesty with identifying marketing as at least half the job and generosity in providing information has been great."

—Kate Wolfe-Jenson, Minnesota,
author of *Dancing with Monsters*

"I've found the people at Wheatmark to be great resources for the latest information on self-publishing, including how to get started marketing your book."

—Nina Atwood, Texas
author of *Temptations of the Single Girl*

"Now I understand what I've been doing wrong. Now I will be able to research my market before spending tons on developing a book that may not have a broad enough range of buyers."

—Dr. Shirley Robinson Sprinkles, Texas
author of *From Dunbar to Destiny*

"Without the exceptional professionalism of Wheatmark . . . I would be stumbling around in the dark. Their experience, excitement, and encouragement put me on the right road towards success."

—Tod Langley, Indiana
author of *Prince Kristian's Honor*

CPSIA information can be obtained
at www.ICGtesting.com
Printed in the USA
BVHW021942190219
540674BV00001B/1/P